# Christmas crafting
## with kids

catherine woram

*photography by*
**polly wreford**

# Christmas crafting
## with kids    35 projects for the festive season

RYLAND
PETERS
& SMALL
LONDON NEW YORK

**Senior designer**  Toni Kay
**Commissioning editor**  Annabel Morgan
**Picture research**  Emily Westlake
**Production**  Gemma Moules
**Art director**  Leslie Harrington
**Publishing director**  Alison Starling

**Stylist**  Catherine Woram

First published in the UK in 2008
This edition published in the UK in 2011
by Ryland Peters and Small
20–21 Jockey's Fields
London WC1R 4BW
www.rylandpeters.com

10 9 8 7 6 5 4 3 2 1

Text, design and photographs
© Ryland Peters & Small 2008, 2011

ISBN: 978-1-84975-138-4

A CIP record for this book is
available from the British Library.

Printed and bound in China

# contents

6 introduction

8 **decorations** pompom tree decorations * cinnamon sticks * paper snowflakes * orange tree decorations * mini tree * paper lanterns * nativity scene * snow globes * christmas stocking * angel tree topper * paperchains * clay decorations * hanging felt stars * beaded decorations * festive bells * christmas crackers * peg-doll angel * tealight holders * gingerbread house * twiggy wreath

70 **gifts** cinnamon biscuits * pot pourri * candle centrepiece * glasses case * peppermint creams * felt egg cosy * button photo frame * orange pomanders * coconut ice * book bag * planted bulbs * chocolate brownies * découpaged tin

102 **cards & wrapping** potato print wrapping paper * stamped gift tags * 3-D christmas cards * felt motif cards * stencilled gift bag

120 templates
124 sources
126 picture credits
127 index
128 acknowledgments

# introduction

If your kids love getting creative with glue, paint or glitter, or if you enjoyed my previous book, *Crafting with Kids*, then *Christmas Crafting with Kids* is the perfect choice for the festive season and is sure to keep your children busy producing a steady stream of gifts, hand-made cards and decorations. From painted clay decorations studded with glitter to jazzy sequinned crackers and even a cute clay nativity scene, there is something to interest any child, and the wide variety of fun projects will appeal to younger children as well as experienced crafters right up to the age of 10 and beyond. Let your kids go wild exploring their creativity and adding their own personal embellishments to the finished items!

Many traditional crafting techniques are covered here, including potato printing, sewing, painting and modelling, and there are also several projects that involve cooking – a favourite pastime for most children. Each project is accompanied by clear and simple step-by-step photographs and there are also suggestions for other items that can be made employing the same technique. Many projects make use of basic household items such as jam jars and egg cartons, which is a great way of recycling them – another activity that's sure to appeal to eco-conscious kids.

One of the most rewarding aspects of the creation of this book (as with its predecessor, *Crafting with Kids*) was seeing just how much all the children enjoyed the crafting process. My daughters (Jessica, aged 11, and Anna, aged 9) helped with many of the projects and were a constant source of inspiration. I am sure you will enjoy making the projects in the book just as much as your children will, and that your friends and relatives will delight in receiving them as Christmas cards and gifts, too.

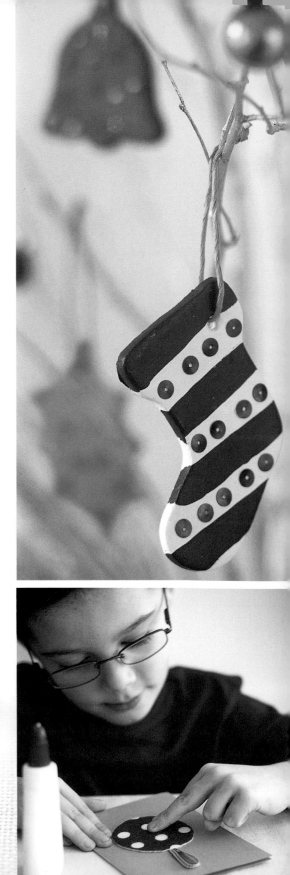

# decorations

**YOU WILL NEED:**

paper • pencil • cardboard • scissors • assorted balls of wool • 3-D fabric pen in red • approx 10cm gingham ribbon per bauble

## wind the wool

Trace the disc template on page 120 onto paper and cut it out. Place it on a piece of cardboard and draw round it. Repeat. Cut out the two discs. Cut a length of wool about 2m long and wind into a small ball that will fit through the hole in the discs. Start to wind wool around the discs, binding them together. When the ball of wool is finished, tie the end to the beginning of a new one. Continue to wind wool round the discs until they are completely covered.

## cut around the outside

When the winding process is complete, hold the pompom discs securely and cut around the edges of the wool using scissors. The wool will fall away looking like fringing at this point, and it is important that the two discs are firmly held together.

## secure the wool

Cut two lengths of wool about 20cm long and thread between the two cardboard discs. Pull them together tightly and knot tightly. The loose ends of this wool will form the hanging loop for the decoration, so tie another knot about 8cm from the first knot and neatly trim the ends.

## finish off

Gently pull the cardboard discs away from the pompom. If it proves difficult, just cut them off. Trim any excess bits of wool, and fluff the pompom to give it a nice round shape. Use a 3-D fabric pen to draw tiny dots on the pompom and finish with a length of red gingham ribbon tied in a bow around the hanging loop.

# pompom
# tree decorations

Pompoms are fun and easy to make, and you can use them to create cute Christmas tree baubles. Alternatively, you could make two different-sized pompoms and glue them together to make a snowman or robin, or even a Father Christmas figure complete with felt hat!

# snowmen

Make one small and one large pompom using white wool and tie the two together using the wool ends. Trim any uneven ends. Now tie a green pipe cleaner around the snowman's neck to create a scarf, and twist a black pipe cleaner into a hat shape. Glue on a triangle of orange felt for a carrot nose, and use a 3-D fabric pen to draw on his eyes and buttons.

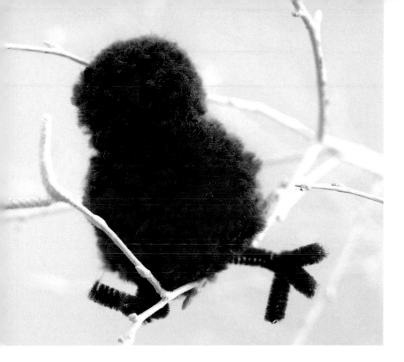

# robin tree decoration

Make a small pompom in brown wool for the head. Now wind red wool around one half of two larger pompom discs and brown wool around the other half. Snip around the edges of the disc and secure the pompom with a length of wool. Use the wool ends to tie the two pompoms together to form a robin. Add a triangle of red felt for his beak and bend brown pipe cleaners into shape for his feet.

# father christmas

Make one large pompom from red wool for the body. To make the head, wind red wool around one half of two smaller pompom discs and white wool around the other half. Snip around the edges of the disc and secure the pompom with a length of wool. Use the wool ends to tie the two pompoms together to form a cuddly Father Christmas figure. Add a hat formed from a quarter-circle of red felt, and a black felt belt. Use a black 3-D fabric pen to draw on his eyes and buttons.

## little tips

Remember: the more wool you manage to wind around the discs, the fatter your pompom will be. For a really plump pompom, try winding the wool around the discs twice.

# cinnamon sticks

A bundle of cinnamon sticks tied together with red gingham ribbon and finished with a tiny jingle bell makes a pretty and fragrant addition to any Christmas tree.

YOU WILL NEED
(for each decoration):
five cinnamon sticks • scissors •
40cm red gingham ribbon
(7mm wide) • 5cm thin wire •
small gold bell

## bundle cinnamon together

Cut a 20cm length of gingham ribbon. Lay it flat on a table and place five cinnamon sticks on top. Wind the ribbon around the sticks once and pull the ends of the ribbon tight.

## arrange ribbon on sticks
Now take the remaining piece of ribbon and lay it on top of the cinnamon sticks, running in the same direction as them, so that the ribbon forms the shape of a cross.

## make hanging loop
Bring the two ends of the first piece of ribbon up from beneath the cinnamon sticks, and knot them on top of the sticks. Now make another knot approx 5cm further up the ribbon. This will form a loop to hang the decoration from.

## finish off
Tie the ends of the second piece of ribbon into a neat bow. Now thread the jingle bell onto the piece of wire, and push the wire through the knot of the bow. Twist the ends of the wire together to secure the bell in place, and trim the wire ends to finish.

YOU WILL NEED:
**square pieces of paper •
pencil • scissors**

## fold paper
Take a square piece of paper. Fold it in half diagonally to form a triangle. Then fold in half again and then into quarters. You should now have a small folded triangle shape.

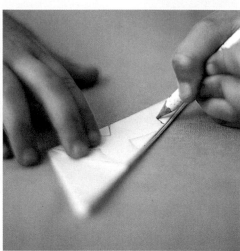

## draw on design
Using the pencil, draw triangular or scalloped shapes on the folded edges of the paper. You can draw curved shapes on the top edges of the paper (furthest from the centre of the paper), too. Experiment with different shapes, so that all your snowflakes are slightly different.

## cut out
Using scissors, carefully cut along the lines you have drawn on the paper. The more shapes you cut out, the more decorative and delicate the finished snowflake will be.

## pull open
Gently unfold the paper and carefully press it flat to reveal the snowflake's design. You can cut snowflakes from any piece of paper, but good sizes are a 20cm square for a large snowflake and a 10cm square for a small one.

# paper snowflakes

Paper snowflakes are so simple to make, yet so effective. Snip them from white paper, tissue paper or tracing paper to create cheap and pretty Christmas decorations. They can be used to decorate windows or suspended from lengths of cotton for a mobile effect. Alternatively, use them to adorn a vase of bare branches to make a striking tabletop decoration.

**YOU WILL NEED:**
fresh oranges • sharp knife •
tea towel • baking tray •
wooden skewer or awl • 15cm
gingham ribbon (10mm wide)
for each hanging loop

**slice the oranges**  Ask an adult to cut the orange slices approximately 5mm wide. Lay the slices on a tea towel and blot them with kitchen towel to remove any excess moisture. This will speed up the drying process.

**bake in oven**  Lay the orange slices on a metal baking tray. Put them in the oven on the very lowest setting and leave them for about four hours or until they are completely dry. The trick is to let them 'cook' long enough to dry completely. If they do not dry entirely, they won't keep for long and may go mouldy. Ask an adult to remove the tray from the oven, as it will be very hot.

**remove dried oranges**  Once the tray has completely cooled, remove the orange slices from the tray and set them aside for decorating. The slices should be hard and dry, but retain their citrussy fragrance.

**finish off**  Ask an adult to make a small hole in the orange using a sharp point such as a wooden skewer. Thread the ribbon through the hole and tie the ends in a knot. Trim the ribbon ends on the diagonal to prevent them from fraying.

# orange tree decorations

Dried orange slices hung from a ribbon loop
make fragrant and unusual tree decorations.
They also make a great addition to our pot
pourri, which can be found on pages 76–77.

# mini tree

Use a real or artificial miniature tree to create a fun and festive centrepiece for the Christmas table. Kids will enjoy decorating it with tiny baubles, miniature pompoms and candy canes made from twisted pipe cleaners.

**YOU WILL NEED:**

miniature Christmas tree • terracotta pot • paintbrushes • undercoat • silver paint • 1m gingham ribbon (25mm wide) • scissors • glue • red and white pipe cleaners • 1m silver ribbon (5mm wide) • red and silver miniature pompoms • 2m gingham ribbon (10mm) wide • miniature baubles (if desired)

**paint pot** Apply a layer of undercoat to the terracotta pot and let it dry completely. Now apply a coat of silver paint and let dry. If necessary, apply a second coat of silver paint for more even coverage, and let it dry.

**attach ribbon and bow** Measure the circumference of the top of the pot and cut a length of the wider gingham to fit. Glue it around the rim of the pot. Tie a neat bow from the same ribbon and glue it to the front of the pot. Let the glue dry.

**make candy canes** Twist the bottom ends of the pipe cleaners together so they are attached. Now wind them together for a striped effect.

**shape canes** Carefully bend one end of the twisted pipe cleaners to form a candy-cane shape with a curved top. Now they can simply be hooked onto the Christmas tree.

**make hanging loop** Cut a 6cm length of the narrow silver ribbon. Fold it in half and pinch the ends together to form a loop. Apply a small dab of glue to hold the ends in place. Let the glue dry.

**attach loop** Using a pair of scissors, carefully snip open a pompom so that you can see the centre. Apply a dab of glue to the middle of the pompom and push in the end of the loop. Press the two sides of the opening closed. Allow the glue to dry completely before hanging the pompoms from the tree.

**tie on bows** Cut lengths of the narrower gingham ribbon and tie them into bows on the ends of the branches of the Christmas tree. Cut the ends of ribbon on the diagonal to prevent them from fraying.

**tie tree topper** Cut a 20cm length of the wider gingham ribbon and tie it around the top of the Christmas tree to make a tree topper. Cut the ends on the diagonal to prevent the ribbon fraying.

## little tips

The red colour scheme we used would work equally well in golds and silvers to create a more luxurious feel for a Christmas table. Or try using all white for an icy winter theme.

**YOU WILL NEED:**
decorative wrapping paper •
scissors • pencil • ruler • glue •
sequin trim to decorate (20cm
per lantern)

**cut and fold paper** Cut a
square of paper measuring 20cm by
20cm for the lantern and a strip of
paper 1.5cm by 20cm for the handle
to hang it from. Fold the square of
paper in half and press flat.

**snip lantern holes** Take the piece of folded paper
and, cutting inwards from the folded edge of the paper, use
scissors to snip flaps that finish about 3cm from the top of the
paper. Each flap should be spaced about 2cm apart. You may
want to mark out the lines using a pencil and a ruler first, to
make it easier to cut the paper properly.

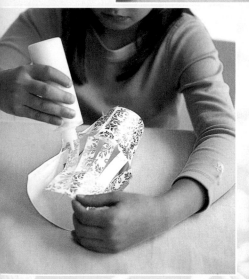

**glue into round** To make the lantern shape, unfold the paper and roll
it to form a tube shape with the paper slits running vertically. Glue the edges
of the paper together to form a round tubular lantern, then press downwards
gently to form a splayed lantern shape.

**finish off** Cut a piece of sequin trim
to fit around the top of the lantern and
glue it in place. Glue the ends of the
hanging loop to the inside of the lantern
on both sides and let dry completely.

# paper lanterns

Paper lanterns are a traditional and fun way of using a piece of paper to make three-dimensional objects. They look very pretty fashioned from soft pink and silver wrapping paper and trimmed with sequins for a festive look. They would also look great in simple red and white trimmed with patterned ribbon.

# nativity scene

A wonderful family keepsake that can be brought out every year, this nativity scene is made from Fimo coloured modelling clay. Each figure is based on a simple tube shape and decorated with touches of gold.

**YOU WILL NEED:**

Fimo modelling clay in assorted colours • small rolling pin • raffia for crib • scissors • Fimo gold dust for decorating • paintbrush

**make baby** Take some white modelling clay and roll out a bean shape about 3cm in length for the baby's body. If the modelling clay is hard, work it between the hands to soften it, so it is easier to mould into shape.

**make face** Take a small piece of flesh-coloured modelling clay and roll it into a ball. Flatten it with your fingers to form a small round disc. Press the disc firmly onto the top of the body shape. Use tiny pieces of black clay to make the eyes and a mouth, and press them into position on the face.

**make crib** Take the brown modelling clay and roll it into a bean shape measuring about 4cm in length and about 1.5cm in diameter. Use your thumb to press down and make an indentation in the crib. Roll two balls of brown modelling clay and press them flat to make the legs of the crib.

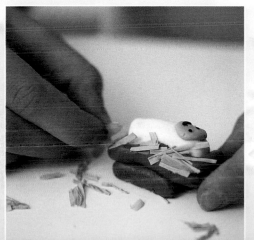

**decorate with raffia** Use scissors to snip small pieces of raffia for the straw in the crib. Press the pieces of raffia firmly against the sides of the crib until they stick in place.

**make other figures** Each figure for the nativity scene is made from a basic bean shape formed from clay and measuring approximately 5cm in length and 1.5cm in diameter. Take a small piece of flesh-coloured clay, roll it into a ball and press it flat to form the face. Using the same method, make a beard from brown clay and use tiny pieces of black clay for the eyes and mouth.

**make cloak** To make the cloak, roll out a piece of clay to approximately 10cm long by 1cm wide. Fold it over the body and press firmly in place. If the cloak is too long, trim the ends with scissors.

**attach arms** Make two small rolls of flesh-coloured clay for the arms and press them firmly against the front of the body. Use more small pieces of clay to form the gifts for the kings to carry, and press them into position between the arms at the front of the body.

**finish off** The kings' gifts and crowns are finished off with fine gold dust applied with a paintbrush. Lay the figure on its side while you apply the dust, to prevent it falling onto the rest of the figure.

# snow globes

Snow globes make great gifts for friends and family, and children really enjoy making them.

**YOU WILL NEED:**

empty, clean jam jars • silver paint • paintbrush • strong waterproof glue or waterproof tile adhesive • Christmas decorations to put in jar • jug and spoon for pouring • distilled water • glycerine • clear washing-up liquid • glitter

**paint lid**  You may wish to sand the metal lid lightly before painting. Paint the lid of the jam jar with silver paint and let it dry completely. If required, apply a second coat of paint for better coverage and again leave to dry.

**attach decoration**  Use strong glue to attach the decoration to the inside of the jam jar lid. If the decoration is on the small side, build up a small mound using waterproof tile adhesive and press the decoration firmly into this. Leave until completely dry.

**fill jar and add glitter**  Use a jug to pour the distilled water into the jam jar. Fill it right up to the brim. Now stir two teaspoons of glycerine and half a teaspoon of washing-up liquid. Add five or six spoonfuls of glitter to the water. White or silver glitter looks most similar to snow, although bright colours like red or green can look very jolly and festive.

**finish off**  Carefully place the lid on the top of the jam jar and screw the lid tightly in place. The jam jar should be watertight, but you may wish to seal it around the edges with a thin layer of silicone sealant, which is available from good craft stores.

# christmas stocking

Create this pretty Shaker-style stocking in cream wool and decorate with a simple heart and mother-of-pearl button. You could make one for each member of the family and tie on card name tags.

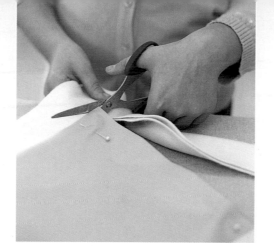

**YOU WILL NEED:**

paper • pencil • scissors • 40cm cream wool fabric (137cm wide) • pins • red felt for heart motif (15cm x 15cm) • needle • white thread • red thread • glue • pearl button • red embroidery thread • 20cm gingham fabric (137cm wide) • 10cm gingham ribbon

## create a template
Trace the stocking template on page 123 onto a piece of paper. Now enlarge it on a photocopier at 200% to make it the right size. Cut out the template. Fold the cream wool fabric in half and pin the template to the fabric. Cut out the stocking pieces.

## cut out heart motif
Trace the heart template on page 123 onto a piece of paper and cut it out. Pin the template to the felt and cut out a heart to decorate the front of the stocking.

## tack heart to stocking
Thread the needle with white cotton and tack the heart motif to the front stocking piece.

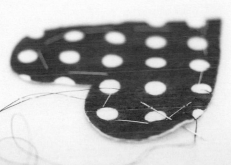

## blanket-stitch heart
Now thread the needle with red cotton and work small blanket stitches all the way around the heart motif. When you have finished, remove the tacking. Now use a dab of glue to stick the pearl button to the centre of the heart.

### stitch stocking together

With right sides facing, tack the two stocking pieces together. Turn right side out. Thread a needle with the red embroidery thread and work blanket stitch all the way around the edges of the stocking, leaving the straight top edges of the stocking open. Press flat using a warm iron (it is advisable for an adult to do this).

### make gingham border

Take the piece of gingham fabric. Fold it in half lengthways, right sides together, and stitch the side seams together using small running stitches. Turn right side out and press flat using an iron (it is advisable for an adult to do this).

### stitch gingham to stocking

Turn a 1cm hem to the inside of the gingham and press flat. Tuck about 8cm of the gingham fabric inside the stocking and fold the remainder of the fabric over the top of the stocking, with the hemmed edge on the outside. Sew small running stitches all around the top of the gingham fabric to hold it in place.

### sew on hanging loop

Fold the piece of gingham ribbon in half to form a loop, and stitch it to the inside of the gingham fabric at the back seam of the stocking.

## little tips

The stocking would work equally well in a bright
Christmassy red colour. Other jolly variations would
be a star or Christmas tree motif on the front of the
stocking. Alternatively, you could write on the
child's name using a 3-D fabric pen.

# angel tree topper

Decorate simple cones of card with a sprinkling of glitter and a pompom to create pretty tree-top angels complete with silver pipe cleaner or feather wings.

**YOU WILL NEED:**

25cm diameter plate as template for cone shape • silver card • pencil • scissors • glue • silver glitter • stapler • silver pipe cleaner • pompom for head • blue and pink 3-D fabric pens for face • gold pipe cleaner

### draw around plate  Place the plate on the silver card and draw around half of it to create a semi-circle for the cone. Cut out.

### apply glitter  Use glue to draw a scalloped line all around the curved edge of the semi-circular piece of card. Sprinkle silver glitter over the glue and leave for a few minutes. Shake off any excess glitter and allow the glue to dry completely.

### form cone shape  Form the card semi-circle into a cone shape (folding it gently in half and making a slight crease at the centre of the card makes it a bit easier to form a cone). Use a stapler to join the card together.

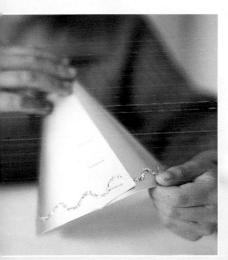

### make wings  Use the silver pipe cleaner to form the wings. Twist the ends over to form a figure of eight.

**attach wings** Apply a dab of glue to the centre of the wings and glue them to the back of the cone, about 3cm down from the top. Allow glue to dry completely.

**glue on pompom head** Use a readymade pompom or make your own following the instructions on pages 10–11. Glue the pompom to the top of the cone and leave to dry.

**draw face** Use 3-D fabric pens in pink and blue to draw the angel's eyes and mouth on the pompom. Leave to dry.

**finish off** For a halo, bend a gold pipe cleaner into a circular shape with a diameter of about 3cm. Twist the ends together to secure, and glue it to the top of the pompom head to finish.

## little tips

Use red card to make a
Father Christmas tree topper
complete with a cotton-wool
beard or a Rudolf the
reindeer tree topper using
brown card and a pair of
pipe cleaner antlers!

# paperchains

Traditional paperchains are easy to make and look great made in festive paper for Christmas. We used decorative gold and silver patterned wrapping paper, but they would work equally well in red and white or even icy blues and silver tones.

**YOU WILL NEED:**
scissors • gold and silver wrapping paper • pencil • ruler • glue • stapler (if desired)

**draw lines on paper** Cut the wrapping paper into pieces that are at least 20cm long. Using a pencil and ruler, draw lines on the back of the paper, making sure that each one is approximately 2cm wide. Repeat with the different coloured paper.

**cut out strips** Use the scissors to cut out the paper strips. It is a good idea to keep the colours separate by making a pile of strips in each colour, so they are easier to select when making the chain.

**form first link** Bend the paper to form a loop and apply a dab of glue to fix it together. Press flat and allow glue to dry. You can use a stapler instead of glue, which is quicker, but the staples will be visible.

**continue making chain** Thread the end of a second paper strip through the first loop and glue the ends together. Continue threading alternate strips of silver and gold paper until you have made the required length of paperchain.

## YOU WILL NEED:

air-drying modelling clay •
rolling pin • snowflake-shaped
cookie cutter • drinking straw
(for piercing hole) • spatula •
paints in desired colours •
saucer for paint • paintbrushes •
glue • glitter • ribbon for
hanging loop (5mm wide)

**roll out clay**  Remove the clay from
its packaging and knead to soften it.
Roll the clay out with a rolling pin. For
smaller snowflakes, the clay should be
about 5mm thick. For larger snowflakes,
the clay should be about 8mm thick.

**cut out shape**  Use the snowflake cookie cutter to cut
the shape from the clay. Carefully remove the excess clay
from around the cutter before lifting it off. Use the end of a
drinking straw to pierce a ribbon hole to hang the snowflake
from. Use a spatula to lift the clay shape and place it on a tray
to dry. When the top is dry, turn the shape over so the other
side can dry completely, too. This prevents the edges from
curling as the clay dries.

**paint and decorate**  Apply a coat of white paint to the top and sides
of each snowflake and allow to dry completely. When dry, paint the other side.
Leave to dry. If necessary, apply a further coat of paint for better coverage.

**finish off**  Apply dots of glue to the
front of the decoration and then sprinkle
silver glitter over the snowflake. Gently
shake off the glitter onto a plate, and
leave to dry. Cut an 8cm length of
ribbon and thread through the hole in
the snowflake. Knot the ends to form a
hanging loop for the decoration.

# clay decorations

Children love working with clay, and
it can be used to create fun festive-
shaped decorations that are then
painted and decorated with glitter,
and threaded onto ribbon to hang
from the tree. Other Christmassy
cookie cutters can be used to make
more decorations, as shown overleaf.

## festive shapes

Bright, bold red, green and white paint gives these simple shapes their punchy effect. They were made with holly-, bell- and stocking-shaped cookie cutters and decorated with single sequins attached with a blob of glue. Coloured string was used to hang them from the branches.

## star gift tag

Use a small star-shaped cookie cutter to make a cute decorative gift tag. Remember to pierce a hole using a drinking straw then, when the clay is dry, paint both sides of the star with silver paint. We used frosty sheer white ribbon to tie the star to the gift.

## little tips

Avoid putting the clay near water, as it will make it sticky and difficult to use. Keep any left-over clay wrapped in plastic in an airtight container for future use. A couple of coats of water-based varnish (applied by an adult) will give the painted clay a longer life.

# hanging felt stars

Cut from red and green felt using pinking shears, these jolly tree decorations are an ideal easy sewing project for little fingers. We decorated the star shapes with pretty buttons and hung them from ricrac braid loops.

**YOU WILL NEED:**

paper • pencil • scissors • coloured felt • pins • pinking shears • 15cm red ricrac per decoration • matching cotton thread • needle • polyester stuffing • glue • assorted pearl buttons (approx 8 per decoration)

**make template**   Trace the star template on page 120 onto paper and cut it out.

**draw around template**   Fold the felt in half, as you will need two star shapes per decoration. Use a pencil to draw around the star motif on the felt fabric (it may be easier if you first pin the star motif to the felt to keep it in place).

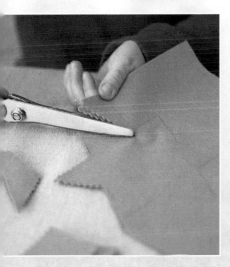

**cut out**   Using pinking shears, carefully cut all the way around the star shape, making sure you are cutting through both layers of fabric. The pinking shears give an attractive zigzag effect to the edges and, if you are using cotton or linen, will prevent the fabric from fraying. If you are making more than one star decoration, it is a good idea to cut them all out at one time.

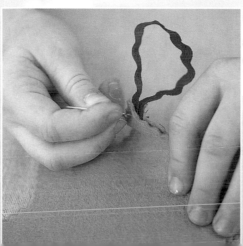

**attach loop**   Fold a 15cm length of ricrac braid in half and place between the two layers of felt at the top of one of the points. Thread the needle. Push the needle through the two layers of felt, sandwiching the loop between them, and make two or three stitches to secure the hanging loop.

## little tips

Use different shapes such as hearts and fill with dried lavender to make cute scented gifts for your family and friends. Sequins or beads can be used instead of buttons for a more festive look.

**stitch together** Continue stitching all the way around the points of the star, using small running stitches about 3mm from the edge. Stitch around five sides of the star but leave the sixth side open for the stuffing.

**stuff heart** Carefully push the stuffing into the opening. You may need to use the end of a knitting needle or a pencil to make sure that the stuffing is pushing right into all the points of the star.

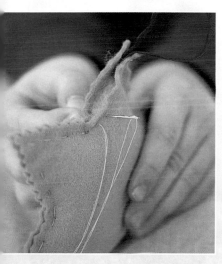

**stitch opening closed** Hold the two layers of felt together and stitch the opening closed, using the same small running stitches about 3mm from the edges of the fabric. Cast off the stitching by making two or three stitches together, and snip the loose ends of the cotton.

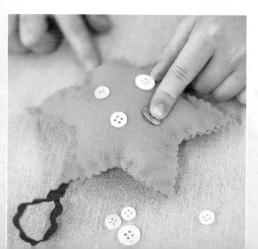

**finish off** Use dabs of glue to stick the buttons to the front of the star decoration and leave to dry completely. You may wish to glue buttons to the other side of the decoration if they are to be hung on a tree, and you will need extra buttons for this.

**YOU WILL NEED:**
wire for hearts (30cm per heart) • glass rocaille beads • pliers (if required) • silver ribbon (5mm wide) • scissors

**thread beads on wire** Fold the wire in half and bend it into a 'V' shape to form the base of the heart. Begin threading beads onto both sides of the wire. Continue threading until all the wire is covered, only leaving about 2cm of bare wire at each end.

**shape into heart** Hold the ends of the wire and bend them inwards to form the curved top of the heart. Twist the ends together to prevent the beads from falling off the wire.

**twist ends of wire** Twist the ends of the wire to form a loop for the ribbon. If the wire is very stiff, it may be advisable for an adult to do this, using a pair of pliers.

**attach hanging loop and bow** Cut a 10cm length of ribbon. Thread it through the wire and knot the ends of the ribbon to form a loop. Trim the ends of the ribbon on the diagonal to prevent them fraying. Cut another length of ribbon about 10cm in length and tie around the wire in a pretty bow to finish.

# beaded decorations

These dainty Christmas tree decorations are fashioned from fine wire threaded with tiny glass rocaille beads and bent into the shape of a heart. They would look good all year round hung from wall hooks or a doorknob.

**YOU WILL NEED:**
a cardboard egg carton •
scissors • pencil • gold and
silver paint • paintbrush •
glue • gold and silver glitter • awl
or wooden skewer • small jingle
bells • 20cm gold or silver cord

**cut out bells** Use scissors to cut the cups from the egg carton. Use a pencil to draw a decorative scalloped line around the bottom edges and cut out, following the line. You could also try cutting the ends with pinking shears for a decorative zigzag effect.

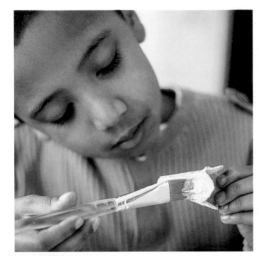

**paint bells** Paint the bells both inside and out and leave to dry. You will need to apply a second coat, as the cardboard will absorb a lot of the paint. Leave the paint to dry completely.

**decorate with glitter** Apply dabs of glue all the way around the bottom of each bell. Sprinkle glitter onto the glue and shake off any excess onto a plate. Leave the glue to dry completely.

**thread bell** Using an awl, pierce a hole in the top of the bell (it is advisable for an adult to do this). Cut a 20cm length of gold or silver cord and thread the bell onto it. Make a knot about 5cm up from the bell, then thread the ends of the cord through the hole in the top of the bell. Tie a knot at the top of the cord to finish.

# festive bells

These festive bells are made from cardboard
egg cartons, which give them their bell-like
shape. To finish, they were painted silver and
gold and decorated with glitter.

# christmas crackers

Making your own crackers is fun and easy, and it means you can put your own choice of novelties and silly handwritten jokes inside. Make the crackers from colourful wrapping paper and trim them with sequins or glitter finished with pretty bows.

**YOU WILL NEED:**

cardboard toilet rolls • 20cm x 30cm piece of paper per cracker • pencil • ruler • scissors • glue or sticky tape • snaps for cracker • gifts, paper hats and jokes • 20cm ribbon (5mm wide) per cracker • sequin trim

**mark paper**   Lay the cardboard roll in the centre of the paper and mark the position of each end using a pencil. Set the roll aside.

**draw lines**   Using the marks made on the paper as a guide, fold the paper in, right sides together, and press the folds flat. Using a ruler, mark out lines along the paper about 1.5cm apart, starting about 2.5cm in from the outside edge of the paper.

**cut slits**   Use scissors to cut along the marked lines to create slits in the paper. Repeat on the other side. These slits enable the cracker ends to be tied more easily.

**roll cracker**   Now unfold the paper and lay it flat. Place the cardboard roll on top. Apply a dab of glue or use a small piece of sticky tape to hold the paper on the roll. Wrap the paper around the roll as tightly as you can.

**glue paper to roll**  Apply glue along the whole edge of the paper and press firmly in place. Allow the glue to dry completely.

**insert snap**  Push the cracker snap through the open end of the roll. This is also the time to insert any small gifts or trinkets, a paper hat, and a joke or other motto.

**tie on ribbon**  Gently tie a 10cm length of ribbon around one end of the cracker. Tie in a knot. Repeat at the other end. Trim the ends of the ribbon on the diagonal with scissors, to prevent them fraying.

**finish off**  Measure the circumference of the cracker and cut three lengths of sequin trim to fit. Glue the sequin trim in rows around the cracker. Allow glue to dry completely.

**YOU WILL NEED:**
pencil • paper • scissors •
wooden clothes peg • white,
silver and yellow paint • fine
paintbrush • black pen •
a paper doily • glue • silver
card • silver pipe cleaner •
sheer ribbon

**make template**  Trace the angel
wing template on page 121 onto paper
and cut it out.

**paint body**  Paint the body of the peg white (this prevents
the wood showing through the holes in the paper doily). Leave
the head of the peg unpainted. Paint the tips of the peg silver
(for the angel's feet) and allow to dry completely.

**draw on face**  Use the yellow paint to give the angel hair, and allow to dry
completely. You may need to apply a second coat of paint for better coverage.
Use the black pen to draw on two eyes and a mouth.

**make robes**  Fold the paper doily in
half and cut along the folded edge. Fold
one half of the doily in half again and cut
a small quarter-circle from the corner, so
that it will fit around the neck of the peg.

# peg-doll angel

Peg dolls make perfect
Christmas decorations
dressed as angels and hung
from the tree. They also
look cute dressed up as
Father Christmas and
wrapped in red felt with
a cotton-wool beard!

**glue on dress**  Wrap the doily around the peg doll and apply a dab of glue at the back of the neck to hold it in place. Now glue all the way along the back of the dress from top to bottom, then leave to dry completely.

**cut out wings**  Use a pencil to draw round the paper wing template on the back of the silver card. Cut the wings out and apply a dab of the glue to the centre of the silver side of the card.

**glue on wings**  Press the wings onto the back of the peg-doll angel, approximately 1cm below the neck. Allow the glue to dry completely.

**finish off**  Wrap the silver pipe cleaner around the angel's head to work out the length required for the halo. Bend the pipe cleaner into a circular halo and twist the ends together. Place on the angel's head and glue in place. Tie a length of ribbon around the neck and knot the ends to form a hanging loop.

# tealight holders

Plain glass tealight holders have been decorated with simple snowflake motifs to create pretty decorations that would make welcome gifts for family and friends. Fill with scented tealights to finish.

YOU WILL NEED:

pencil • paper • scissors •
masking tape • glass tealight
holders • 3-D fabric pens

**draw motif**  Trace the snowflake motif on page 123 onto paper. Cut the paper into a small square that will fit inside the tealight holder.

**place motif in glass**  Place the paper motif inside the glass tealight holder and use small pieces of masking tape to hold it in place. The design should face outwards so it is clearly visible through the glass of the holder.

**fill in motif**  Starting from the centre, using a 3-D fabric pen, draw small dots approximately 2mm apart all the way along the lines of the snowflake stencil. Be careful not to smudge the paint as you work – it takes about an hour to dry completely.

**finish off**  Continue filling in the dots along the lines of the stencil, then allow the paint to dry completely. You could experiment with other patterns, such as a simple row of dots around the rim of the tealight holder. When the paint has dried, drop a coloured or scented tealight inside each holder.

# gingerbread house

This decorative and delicious gingerbread house makes a fabulous table centrepiece for Christmas and will elicit oohs and aahs of admiration when it is unveiled! We decorated the plain gingerbread with white icing, sweets and candy canes, as well as silver sugar balls.

## YOU WILL NEED:

5 baking trays • baking parchment • 225g plain flour, plus extra for dusting • 1 tsp ground ginger • 1 tsp ground cinnamon • 1 tsp bicarbonate of soda • 60g butter • 2 tbsp dark brown sugar • 80g golden syrup • 1 tbsp beaten egg • rolling pin • rectangular foiled cake board • icing sugar • silver balls • tubes of icing • 2 red jelly sweets • rock candy canes • small red and white sweets to decorate

### mix ingredients
Preheat the oven to 190°C (375°F) Gas 5 and cover five baking trays with baking parchment. Now sieve the flour, ginger, cinnamon and bicarbonate of soda into the bowl of an electric mixer or a food processor. Add the butter and whizz until the mixture resembles fine breadcrumbs

### add sugar and syrup
Now add the brown sugar, golden syrup and egg to the mixer bowl and blitz to form a soft dough. If the consistency is too dry, add a little more egg.

### roll out the dough
Roll the dough out to an 8–10mm thickness, so that it is firm enough to hold its shape once cooked. Cut out two large rectangles for the roof, two smaller rectangular side panels, and a front and back section with a pointed gable. Use the template on page 122 for the front and back section.

### place on baking tray
Carefully lay the pieces of the gingerbread house on separate baking trays. Bake for 8–10 minutes until a light golden brown in colour. Leave on the baking trays until firm to the touch, then transfer to a rack to cool.

**build the house** Make up some icing following the instructions on the packet. The consistency should be thick enough to 'glue' the gingerbread together. Spread icing along the front of the cake board and stand the front section of the house on top. When it is stable, apply more icing to one end of the side walls and stick them to the front section. Hold the two pieces in place until secure. Now attach the back section to the other ends of the walls. Let the icing dry completely.

**decorate the roof** Use a ready-mixed tube of icing to pipe a scalloped tiled pattern to the roof. Decorate the icing with silver balls and let dry completely. Repeat for the other section of the roof, and let dry.

**finish off** Pipe on the windows using the tube of icing. Pipe a door shape on the front section, then stick rock candy pieces to the icing. Use icing to attach sweets around the edges of the house. Apply more icing to the edges of the house, and carefully place the roof in position. Hold in place until the icing holds (you may have to use cocktail sticks to hold it in position from beneath). When the icing is completely dry, decorate the roof ridge with rock candy and add two sweets as chimneys.

## little tips

Try using any left-over gingerbread mixture to make tiny gingerbread figures to place outside the house. You can decorate them with icing to create cute Father Christmas figures, cheery snowmen or jolly reindeer!

# twiggy wreath

Make this decorative door wreath from natural twigs and decorate with dried leaves painted silver and gold. Hang it on the front door, or lay it flat on a table and fill the centre with candles for a striking table decoration.

**YOU WILL NEED:**

assortment of natural-coloured twigs • 25cm diameter florist's wire ring • string • scissors • dried leaves in assorted shapes • gold and silver paint • paintbrush • glue • 50cm gold ribbon (30mm wide) for bow

**tie on twigs**  Carefully bend the twigs in place around the wire ring and use short lengths of string to tie them in place. Continue until the wire ring is completely covered with and concealed by the twigs. Trim any very long twigs with scissors.

**paint leaves**  Lay the dried leaves facing upwards on a large piece of paper and paint each one with gold or silver paint. Let them dry thoroughly and apply a further coat to each leaf if better coverage is required.

**glue on leaves**  Apply three or four dabs of glue to the back of a leaf and stick it to the twigs. Continue to glue on the leaves, placing them at regular intervals and alternating between silver and gold, until the wreath is covered with a layer of painted leaves.

**finish off**  Tie the length of gold ribbon at the top of the wreath and make a bow. Trim the ends of the ribbon on the diagonal to prevent them from fraying.

# gifts

# cinnamon biscuits

These yummy biscuits decorated with icing and silver balls make perfect gifts for teachers, neighbours or other grown-ups. You could also hang them from lengths of festive ribbon to make pretty tree decorations.

YOU WILL NEED:

225g plain flour, plus extra for dusting • 1 tsp ground cinnamon • 1 tsp ground ginger • 1tsp bicarbonate of soda • 60g butter • 2 tbsps dark brown sugar • 80g golden syrup • 1tbsp beaten egg • rolling pin • star-shaped cookie cutter • drinking straw • baking tray • icing sugar, silver balls and other decorations of your choice • narrow ribbon

**MAKES 25 SMALL COOKIES**

**get started** Preheat the oven to 190°C (375°F) Gas 5. Cover two baking trays with baking parchment.

**add the flour** Sift the flour, cinnamon, ginger, and bicarbonate of soda into a wide bowl or a food processor. Add the butter and mix thoroughly with a wooden spoon or whizz in the processor until the mixture resembles fine breadcrumbs.

**form dough** Add the sugar, golden syrup and egg and mix together or blitz in the food processor to make a soft dough. If it feels too dry, add a little more egg. Now form the dough into a ball then flatten it out so it is ready for rolling.

**roll out dough** Using a small rolling pin, carefully and evenly roll out the dough to a thickness of about 5mm.

**cut out biscuits** Using star-shaped cookie cutters, cut out the biscuits. Use a drinking straw to punch a small hanging hole in each biscuit, about 1cm from the edge. Place the biscuits on the baking tray. Bake them in the oven for 8–10 minutes until light golden brown.

**make icing** Leave the baked cookies on the trays until they are firm, then transfer to a rack to cool. To decorate the biscuits, you can either use ready-mixed icing, which is available in tubes and bottles, or make your own by beating together icing sugar and water to create a thin icing (you can add food colouring to the icing for more colourful effects).

**decorate biscuits** Use the icing sugar to decorate the biscuits, then add more decorations. Silver and gold sugar balls look suitably festive on Christmas biscuits, and you can try adding coloured sugar and other pretty sprinkles too.

**finish off** Once the decorations have dried completely, thread a length of narrow ribbon through the hole in each biscuit. If you can resist eating them, they are now ready to be boxed up as gifts or hung from the Christmas tree!

YOU WILL NEED:

pine cones, cinnamon sticks and dried orange slices (see pages 18–19) • cellophane bags • air-drying clay • small heart-shaped cookie cutter • drinking straw • green paint • paintbrush • 20cm narrow gingham ribbon (10mm wide) • 30cm gingham ribbon (20mm wide)

**fill bag**  Make the dried orange slices following the instructions on page 18–19. Put the cones, cinnamon sticks and orange slices into a bowl. Now fill the cellophane bag with the pot pourri, layering the different items for an attractive effect.

**paint clay decorations**  Following the instructions on page 42-43, make two clay hearts per bag of pot pourri. Use a heart-shaped cookie cutter to cut them out, and use a drinking straw to pierce a hole in each one to thread the ribbon through. Let dry, then paint the hearts green on both sides.

**tie on clay decorations**  Thread the narrow ribbon through the holes of one heart and tie a knot at the back of the heart to prevent it slipping off. Tie the narrow ribbon around the neck of the bag and draw tight. Now tie the wider ribbon together around the ends of the narrow ribbon, just below the knot.

**finish off**  Tie the wider ribbon in a bow around the cellophane. Tease the top of the cellophane bag so that it sticks out attractively. Trim the ends of the ribbon on the diagonal to prevent the ends from fraying.

# pot pourri

Pot pourri is fun and easy to make and is always a welcome gift. It looks very pretty wrapped in a glossy cellophane bag and decorated with ribbon and heart-shaped clay decorations.

# candle centrepiece

A simple terracotta flowerpot painted silver, decorated with ivy leaves and holding a simple pillar candle makes a simple yet effective centrepiece for the Christmas table. Group them together in a row of three for a more dramatic effect.

**YOU WILL NEED:**

terracotta flowerpot (15cm diameter) • undercoat • silver paint • paintbrushes • double-sided sticky tape • 50cm sheer silver ribbon (25mm wide) • pillar candle (approx 20cm tall) • sand or fine gravel • fresh or artificial ivy leaves

**paint flowerpot** Apply a coat of undercoat to the terracotta pot and leave to dry completely. Now apply a coat of silver paint and let dry. Paint the inside of the pot and leave to dry. If necessary, apply a further coat of paint for better coverage, then allow to dry completely.

**tie on bow** Place a small piece of double-sided sticky tape at the back of the pot on the rim and press the centre of the ribbon onto this so it is securely fixed in place. Tie the ribbon into a decorative bow at the front of the pot. Trim the ends of the ribbon on the diagonal to prevent the ends from fraying.

**add candle** Place the candle in the terracotta pot. If it is slightly wobbly, you may find it easier to put some sand or fine gravel in the bottom of the pot to support the candle and hold it in place. Remember to cover the hole in the base of the pot with a piece of sticky tape first!

**finish off** Use fresh or artificial ivy leaves to decorate around the rim of the pot. You will need to use a dab of glue to hold them in place. If the pot is intended as a gift, it is better to use artificial leaves, as they will last longer.

## create a template

Trace the glasses case template on page 122 onto paper and cut it out. Fold the felt in half, with right sides facing, place the paper template on the wrong side of the felt, and draw all the way around the template using a pencil. It may be easier if you pin the template to the felt before you draw around it.

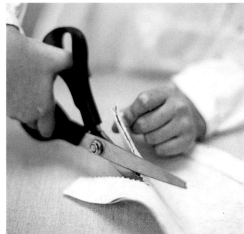

## cut out fabric

Firmly holding the two layers of felt together, use pinking shears to cut out the glasses case.

## stitch pieces together

Thread a needle with the embroidery thread and, with wrong sides of the fabric facing, use simple running stitch of about 1cm width to sew all the way around the outside edge of the case. Leave the top straight edge of the glasses case open.

## finish off

Take the length of ricrac and place one end at the centre back of the glasses case approximately 1.5cm below the open edge. Apply a dab of glue to the end of the ricrac, then apply a thin line of glue to the back of the ricrac braid, and press down to secure it to the glasses case. Allow the glue to dry completely.

# glasses case

A great gift for grandparents, this fun glasses case is quick and easy to make from polka-dot felt and ricrac braid in jolly colours.

**YOU WILL NEED:**

500g icing sugar • 4 tbsps condensed milk • oil of peppermint • miniature silver petit-four cases • pale blue ready-rolled icing • ready-mixed tubes of black and brown icing

**MAKES 16 SNOWMEN**

**mix ingredients**  Sift the icing sugar into a bowl and stir in the condensed milk until the mixture becomes a smooth paste. Add three drops of oil of peppermint and knead it into the mixture until the flavour is thoroughly worked through. Add more oil of peppermint a drop at a time and knead it in thoroughly until you achieve the desired intensity of flavour.

**form snowmen**  Roll the mixture between the palms of your hands to form the ball for the bottom half of the snowman. Place in a silver petit-four case and then roll a smaller ball for the head. Place the head gently on top of the larger ball and push down to secure.

**add scarves**  Roll out the pale blue icing. Ask an adult to use a sharp knife to cut lengths measuring about 3mm wide by 10cm long. Wrap one around the neck of each snowman to form a scarf.

**finish off**  Use ready-mixed black icing to form the snowmen's hats and eyes. To finish, roll blobs of brown icing into tiny balls for the snowmen's noses and stick them firmly in place. Let the snowmen dry completely before packaging them up.

# peppermint creams

Delicious to eat and oh-so-easy to make, peppermint creams make great gifts and the mixture can be used to form fun shapes, such as these cute snowmen with their black icing hats and snug blue scarves!

# felt egg cosy

This cute, colourful felt egg cosy is easy
to make and makes a great gift. Younger
children who are not quite as proficient
at sewing may need some
help with the stitching.
You can also use glue
to attach the motif
shape to the cosy.

**YOU WILL NEED:**
paper • pencil • pins •
scissors • felt in two
different colours • cookie
cutters to use as stencils for
motifs • sewing thread in
two different colours •
needle • glue • pretty
buttons to decorate

**create template** Trace the egg
cosy template on page 121 onto a
piece of plain paper and cut it out.
Pin the template to the fabric and cut
out two shapes. Now use a cookie
cutter to cut out a star (or tree) motif
from the different-coloured felt.

**stitch on motif** Using small blanket stitches in
contrasting thread, stitch the felt motif to the front of one
of the the egg cosy pieces. Use two strands of thread to
make the stitches more visible. Younger children may find
it easier to glue the motif to the egg cosy.

**stitch together** Place the two egg cosy pieces with right sides facing.
Stitch the back and front of the egg cosy together using blanket stitch.
When you have finished stitching around the sides, continue the blanket
stitch along the open bottom edges of the egg cosy.

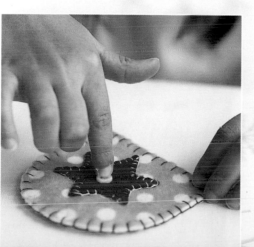

**finish off** Decorate the felt motifs
using pretty mother-of-pearl buttons.
Use a small dab of glue on the back
of each button and stick it to the felt
motif to finish.

YOU WILL NEED:

plain wood picture frame • red or green paint • paintbrushes • assorted red buttons in different shapes and sizes, but approx 10mm in diameter • glue • coloured pencils • paper

**paint frame**  Paint the wooden frame using your chosen colour of paint and let it dry completely. If necessary, apply a further coat of paint for better coverage, then allow to dry completely.

**glue buttons to corners**  Glue a button to each corner of the frame and press down firmly to make sure that they are firmly stuck in place. You may wish to use buttons in an assortment of bright colours. Alternatively, mother-of-pearl buttons can look very pretty.

**continue to glue on buttons**  Continue to glue on the rest of the buttons, working all the way around the frame and alternating different sizes and shapes. Press down hard on each button as you glue it in place to make sure that it is secure. Leave to dry completely.

**draw pictures**  Use coloured pencils to draw a festive picture to insert in the finished frame – Christmas trees, stars, bells or Father Christmas would all look great.

# button photo frame

Painted in festive red and green and decorated with jolly buttons, this fun photo frame makes a great gift for a granny or grandpa, especially when used to display children's own artwork.

# orange pomanders

These traditional pomanders made from oranges and decorated with cloves have long been associated with Christmas. Their sweet, spicy smell makes them welcome gifts for family and friends, or pretty decorations to hang in the home.

YOU WILL NEED:
biro • large orange • bradawl
(for piercing holes) • cloves •
60cm ribbon (10mm wide) •
scissors • pin

**mark ribbon positions** Use
the biro to mark out the ribbon positions
around the orange. The ribbon is wrapped
round the orange in the shape of a cross.
Use the bradawl to pierce holes for the
cloves on the four quarters of the orange.
Bradawls are very sharp, so it is advisable
for an adult to pierce the holes.

**insert cloves** Carefully push the cloves into the orange.
The tops of the cloves tend to be quite brittle, so push them
in gently. Continue to push the cloves into the orange until
all four quarters are covered.

**fix ribbon** Wrap a length of ribbon around the orange so the ends overlap
at the bottom of the orange. Snip the ribbon and hold the first piece in place
as you wrap another length around the orange. Trim any trailing ribbon ends.
Now push a pin through the ends of the ribbon to hold it in place.

**finish off** Thread a length of ribbon
through the top of the crossed ribbon
on the orange and tie the ends together.
Tie a knot in the ribbon about 5cm from
the top of the orange to form a loop.
Now thread a further length of ribbon
through the top of the ribbon and tie
into a pretty bow to finish.

YOU WILL NEED:

750g icing sugar, sifted, plus extra for dusting •
250ml canned sweetened condensed milk •
375g desiccated coconut • 2 tbsps freshly
squeezed lemon juice • 3-4 drops vanilla essence •
5–6 drops pink food colouring • rolling pin • baking
sheet, 28cm x 18cm x 4cm, lined with baking
parchment and lightly dusted with icing sugar •
cookie cutters in festive shapes • sieve

**MAKES ABOUT 40 PIECES OR 10 BARS**

## mix ingredients
Put the sifted icing sugar into a large
bowl, add the condensed milk and mix with a wooden spoon
until smooth.  Add the coconut, lemon juice and vanilla and stir
to form a stiff paste. Add the pink food colouring and mix well
until the colour is evenly worked through.

## roll out mixture
Let the mixture set for about half an
hour so that it becomes firmer. Sprinkle the rolling surface with
icing sugar and roll out the mixture using a rolling pin. Sprinkle
icing sugar on top of the mixture as you are rolling it, to prevent
the rolling pin from sticking.

## cut out shapes
Use the cookie cutters to cut out shapes from the
coconut ice mixture. Place the shapes on a baking sheet covered with
baking parchment to dry.

## finish off
Sift icing sugar over the
coconut ice to create a pretty frosted
effect. You may also wish to add other
decorations such as silver sugar balls.
Coconut ice can be stored in an airtight
container for about two weeks.

# coconut ice

Deliciously sweet as well as irresistibly pretty, coconut ice is fun and easy for kids to make, and can be cut into decorative festive shapes. This homemade version is much more delicious than shop-bought varieties.

# book bag

This pretty but practical wool book bag is decorated with a very simple festive Christmas tree motif formed from lengths of silver ricrac. It makes a lovely gift for a school friend or a younger family member.

**YOU WILL NEED:**

30cm wool fabric (137cm width) • pinking shears • needle • white wool for stitching • silver ricrac braid • scissors • glue • scraps of decorative white felt for pot and bauble motifs

**sew hem at top of bag**  Using pinking shears, cut a length of wool fabric measuring 55cm long by 24cm wide. Fold over the shorter ends by 1cm and work running stitches along this edge. The stitches you make should be approximately 1cm in width.

**continue sewing backwards**  When you have finished, start stitching backwards over the existing stitches, so that there are no gaps. Repeat at the other end of the bag, then press the hems flat using a warm iron (it is advisable for an adult to do this).

**stitch sides together**  Fold the piece of fabric in half widthways with wrong sides facing and stitch along the two side edges using the same stitching technique used for the hem.

**cut lengths of ricrac**  Cut nine lengths of silver ricrac braid in the following measurements: 16cm, 14cm, 12cm, 8cm, 6cm 4cm, 3cm 2cm and 1cm. Try to cut the ends of the ric rac diagonally with the scissors, to prevent the ends from fraying.

**glue on ricrac**  Begin by applying a thin line of glue to the back of the longest length of ricrac. Carefully lay it on the fabric towards the bottom of the bag about 7cm up from the base. Press down flat using your fingers. Continue to stick on the remaining lengths of ricrac in order of length, each about 1.5cm apart, to form the Christmas tree shape.

**glue on pot**  Cut out the pot shape and circular bauble for the top of the tree from felt. Glue to the top and base of the ricrac tree shape and allow to dry completely.

**make handles**  Cut two lengths of wool fabric measuring 33cm by 6.5cm for the handles. Fold one of the longer edges over by 2cm and the remaining side over the top of this by 1.5cm and press flat. Stitch down the centre of each handle using running stitch and press flat using a warm iron (it is advisable for an adult to do this).

**finish off**  Stitch one handle to the inside of the bag, working approximately 4cm down from the opening and using neat whipping stitches to secure in place. Repeat with the other handle on the other side of the bag to finish.

# cushion

We used pale green wool fabric to make this cute cushion decorated with a ricrac Christmas tree. This would work equally well in red wool fabric decorated with white or green ricrac braid. The cushion is made using a 30cm square piece of wool fabric and the back is made using two rectangles of wool, each measuring 30cm by 18cm to allow for the back opening.

## planted bulbs

Fragrant and decorative, planted bulbs are a welcome reminder that the warmer spring months lie ahead. They look particularly appealing in a painted terracotta pot tied with ricrac braid and felt decorations.

YOU WILL NEED:
terracotta pot • silver paint •
paintbrush • scissors • double-
sided sticky tape • 70cm red
ricrac braid • felt star
decoration • flowering bulbs
of your choice • compost

**paint pot** Paint the flowerpot using silver paint and leave it to dry. Paint the inside of the pot from the rim to a depth of about 4cm. If necessary, apply a further coat of paint for better coverage, then allow to dry completely.

**tie on ricrac braid** Cut a small square of double-sided sticky tape and stick it at the back of the pot on the rim. Fold the length of ricrac braid in half to find the central point, then open it out and fix the centre of the braid on the piece of sticky tape. Bring the ends of the ricrac around to the front of the pot and tie in a pretty bow.

**add decoration** Use scissors to trim the ends of the braid. Using its hanging loop, tie the felt star decoration to the centre of the ricrac bow and firmly knot in position.

**finish off** Remove the bulbs from their plastic pots and very carefully repot them in the terracotta pot. You may need to add some extra compost to the bottom of the pot first. Gently push the bulbs down into the pot and give them a drink of water to finish.

## YOU WILL NEED:

kitchen foil • 20cm square cake tin • 140g unsalted butter • 4 large eggs • 320g caster sugar • 1 teaspoon vanilla essence • 75g cocoa powder • 140g plain flour • 100g milk chocolate • paper for stencil • icing sugar to decorate

**MAKES 16 BROWNIES**

**mix ingredients**  Preheat the oven to 160°C (325°F) Gas 3. Cut kitchen foil into a 25cm square, then press it into the cake tin to line the base and sides. Melt the butter in a saucepan over a low heat. Crack the eggs into a mixing bowl. Tip in the sugar, then add the vanilla. Stir well with a wooden spoon. Pour in the melted butter and stir. Set a sieve over the mixing bowl and sift the cocoa and flour onto the egg mixture. Stir well.

**add chocolate**  Break the chocolate into small chunks and add to the bowl. Stir until just mixed, then spoon the mixture into the foil-lined tin. Ask an adult to help you put the brownie mix into the oven. They will take about 40 minutes to cook in the centre of the oven. To test if they are ready, push a cocktail stick into one, then pull it out. If the stick is clean, then they are ready; if it's sticky, leave them for another 5 minutes.

**cut out stencil**  Ask an adult to remove the tin from the oven, as it will be very hot. Leave the tin to cool on a wire rack. When completely cold, remove the brownies from the tin, peel off the foil and cut into 16 squares. Trace the Christmas tree stencil on page 122 onto paper and cut out the Christmas tree shape. This is your stencil.

**finish off**  Place the stencil on top of a chocolate brownie and sieve icing sugar over the stencil and brownie. Carefully remove the stencil to reveal the Christmas tree motif. Repeat until all the brownies are decorated.

# chocolate brownies

These delicious chocolate brownies filled with chunks of chocolate are given a festive touch with stencilled Christmas-tree motifs made using sifted icing sugar. If you can resist the temptation, they make great gifts for teachers, family and friends.

**YOU WILL NEED:**

plain biscuit tin or cake tin •
red paint • paintbrush •
assorted scraps of wrapping
paper • scissors • glue •
acrylic varnish (if desired)

**paint tin**  Paint the tin inside and out using the red paint, then leave it to dry. If necessary, apply a further coat of paint for better coverage, then allow the tin to dry completely.

**cut paper pieces**  Cut the wrapping paper into small squares and shapes using the designs of the paper as a guide. Experiment by laying out the shapes on the top of the tin lid so you can work out how many pieces of paper you will need.

**découpage lid**  Start by sticking the pieces of paper to the corner of the lid. If the corners of the lid are curved, you will need to cut curved corners with scissors to fit. Continue to stick pieces of the paper all over the lid until the painted area is completely covered. Once the lid is finished, leave to dry completely.

**finish off**  When you have finished the lid, start sticking smaller motifs such as Christmas trees all the way around the sides of the tin. Leave the tin to dry completely. You may wish to apply a couple of coats of acrylic varnish to the tin to make it more hard-wearing. Allow to dry completely.

# découpaged tin

Scraps of decorative wrapping paper glued to a plain tin create a fantastic presentation box for home-baked Christmas goodies such as cakes, biscuits or brownies. Yum!

# cards & wrapping

YOU WILL NEED:

medium-sized potato •
star-shaped cookie cutter •
chopping board • sharp knife
(to be used by an adult only) •
kitchen paper or dry cloth •
paints in your chosen colours •
saucers to hold the paints •
sponge paint roller • plain
white paper

### cut out shape
Cut the potato in half, making sure the surface of the potato is as flat as possible. Place the cookie cutter on a cutting board with the sharp edge facing upwards. Press the potato firmly down onto the cutter, leaving the cookie cutter standing proud of the cut surface of the potato by about 5mm, so you can cut around it.

### cut away edges
Ask an adult to cut away the edges of the potato using a sharp knife. This needs to be done very carefully, to ensure the star shape is as clear as possible. Press the potato down onto a dry cloth or piece of kitchen paper to remove any excess moisture, which can make the paint watery.

### apply paint
Pour the paint into a saucer and use the end of the sponge paint roller to apply the paint to the star shape. Don't apply too much paint to the potato, as this will make the design bleed. If you have applied too much paint, gently blot the potato on kitchen paper to remove the excess.

### get printing
Begin printing. To ensure the design prints clearly, use a gentle rocking motion, moving the potato from side to side without lifting it from the paper. This will apply the paint evenly, even if the cut surface of the potato is not flat. Continue to print the stars at evenly spaced intervals. Allow the paint to dry completely.

# potato print wrapping paper

Potato printing is a traditional painting technique that is a favourite with kids of all ages. They can use cookie cutters to create pretty shapes, or an adult could use a sharp knife to cut out different shapes by hand.

# stamped gift bag

Use a large potato and a tree-shaped cookie cutter to decorate a paper bag and a matching gift tag to match. We used blobs of glue sprinkled with silver glitter to create the silver bauble effect on the trees and the pretty border along the top edge of the bag.

# holly cards

A holly-shaped cookie cutter was used to create this festive design. It was then stamped onto plain brightly coloured pieces of card to create funky Christmas cards. Decorated with blobs of glue and a sprinkling of silver glitter, the end result looks both fun and festive.

## little tips

Potato printing also looks very effective when carried out on fabric – but make sure you use fabric or stencil paint so the item can be washed. Follow the manufacturer's instructions to 'fix' the fabric paint, as some fabric paints must be fixed with a hot iron.

## stamped gift tags

These pretty gift tags are made using rubber stamps featuring decorative designs. You can make your own tags using a plain card, a hole punch and string ties. The stamped designs work equally well on gift cards and wrapping paper.

**YOU WILL NEED:**
card for tag • scissors • foam pad • stamping ink • rubber stamp • glue • hole punch • plain white paper • 15cm string per tag

**cut out gift tag** Cut out a rectangle of card measuring about 8cm by 15cm. Use scissors to snip off the top two corners of the card on the diagonal, to form the top of the gift tag.

**apply printing ink** Cut out small pieces of white paper measuring about 5cm by 8cm. Using the foam pad, apply some stamping ink to the front of the stamp, making sure the design is completely and evenly covered.

**stamp motif** Place the stamp firmly on the centre of a piece of white paper and use a gentle rocking motion to make sure that the design is completely transferred onto the paper. Leave to dry completely.

**finish off** Glue the paper design to the front of the tag. Use a hole punch to make a hole between the two angled corners of the tag. Thread the string through the hole in the tag to finish.

**YOU WILL NEED:**
paper • pencil • scissors •
blank cards • scraps of
wallpaper or decorative
wrapping paper for motifs •
pinking shears • glue

**create template** Trace the star template on page 120 onto a piece of plain paper and cut it out. Place the template on the back of the decorative paper, and draw around it. You will need two paper shapes per card.

**cut out motifs** Use the pinking shears to carefully cut out the star motifs (you could use other decorative-edged scissors for different effects). See overleaf for more ideas for different festive motifs.

**make centre fold** Take one of the paper star motifs and fold in half, with the right side of the paper facing inwards. Press down this fold. This is the 3-D element of the star on the front of the card.

**finish off** Glue the unfolded star to the front of the card, making sure that all the corners are firmly stuck down. Now dab glue all the way down the fold on the back of the second star, and stick it on top of the first star. When the glue is dry, gently fold the corners outwards to create a 3-D effect.

# 3-D christmas cards

Simple yet effective, these gorgeous 3-D cards can be made using scraps of decorative wallpaper or offcuts of wrapping paper cut into festive shapes then glued to plain cards.

# gold and silver hearts

Use the heart template on page 120 to cut out small and medium-sized hearts from metallic wrapping paper, using pinking shears for a decorative effect. Glue the hearts onto gold and silver cards and finish them off with dainty bows made from gold ribbon.

## blue bells

Simple bell shapes cut from blue and white paper (using the template on page 121) create a pretty, punchy effect on plain white cards. They are topped with sheer white and blue ribbon bows to finish.

## glittery trees

Use the template on page 121 to snip Christmas tree shapes from pretty sugar-pink and silver patterned wrapping paper. The trees are finished off with sparkling 'baubles' – pale pink and silver sequins glued to the ends of the branches.

### little tips

Instead of buying whole sheets of wrapping paper, visit a craft shop and buy a pack of craft paper. These packs include an assortment of decorative printed and embroidered papers that are the perfect size for making the cards here. Scraps of wallpaper also work well, as they are thicker than wrapping paper, which makes them ideal for 3-D shapes.

**YOU WILL NEED:**
round cookie cutter • felt
squares • pencil • scissors •
15cm gingham ribbon (6mm
wide) • glue • blank cards

**cut out felt motif**  Use the circular cookie cutter (or a similar object) as a template for the round bauble shape on this card. Place it on the felt and draw round it with a pencil. Carefully cut out the bauble shape. If you are making more than one card, it's a good idea to cut out all your felt shapes at the same time.

**glue on hanging loop**  Cut a piece of gingham ribbon about 5cm long and fold it into a loop. Glue the ribbon onto the card just below where the top of the bauble will be positioned. Press down firmly to secure it in place.

**stick on felt shape**  Apply a thin layer of glue to the back of the felt bauble shape and stick it onto the card, making sure that you have covered both the ends of the ribbon loop. Press down firmly and allow to dry completely.

**finish off**  Make a ribbon bow from the gingham ribbon. Apply a small dab of glue to the back of the bow, and stick to the front of the bauble. Press down firmly to secure it in place and leave to dry completely.

# felt motif cards

Felt is great for decorating cards, as it comes in a wide selection of colours and does not fray once it is cut. We used Christmas-themed cookie cutters as templates for a variety of festive designs. Glue the felt shapes onto stiff card and finish them off with dainty ribbon bows.

## christmas trees

Christmas tree cookie cutters were used to cut out these shapes from plain red, white and lime green felt. They were glued to cards, then decorated with tiny dots made using 3-D fabric pens.

## glitter stars

Felt stars in plain and patterned felt adorn these square Christmas cards. We added a scattering of silver glitter glue dots for added decoration.

## little tips

Some craft shops sell adhesive-backed felt, which is easier for younger children to use. Draw your chosen design on the backing paper, then cut it out with scissors. Peel off the backing paper, stick the felt onto the greetings card, and decorate to finish.

## YOU WILL NEED:

red wrapping paper • stencil for motif • white paint • stencil brush • kitchen paper • double-sided sticky tape • cardboard • hole punch • 40cm gingham ribbon (12mm wide)

**fold paper** Cut a rectangular piece of red paper measuring 56cm by 33cm. Fold in 4cm along one long edge, and 7cm along the other long edge. Fold in the shorter ends by 1.5cm. Now fold the paper in half so the shorter edges meet, and press flat. Open out again, and on the wrong side of the paper, draw three lines, one 12cm in from one shorter edge, then another at 30cm and a final one at 39cm from the edge. Fold the paper along each line. These folds form the box shape of the bag.

**stencil motif** Dip the brush in the paint and blot on kitchen paper to remove any excess paint. If there is too much paint on the brush, the outline will bleed. Hold the stencil over one of the larger panels of the bag (this will be the front) and dab on the paint. Let the paint dry slightly before removing the stencil.

**fold side edge** Open out the bottom fold of the bag, but keep the top 4cm fold in place. Place some double-sided sticky tape along one edge of the bag and press the other edge onto it to form a square bag shape. Press firmly down.

**fold corners for base** Open out the bag, turn it upside down and fold in the long sides to the middle. Fold the corners into triangles, and use double-sided sticky tape to secure them. Cut a piece of card to fit the base and place it inside the bag to strengthen it. Punch two holes on the front and back of the bag just below the top edge and thread two 20cm lengths of ribbon through them. Knot the ends to hold them in place.

# stencilled gift bag

What better than to present a hand-made gift in your very own hand-crafted gift bag? These were made from plain wrapping paper and stencilled with a Christmassy candy cane design.

# templates

small heart for
centre of
3-D card
(page 112)

heart for
3-D card
(page 112)

star for 3-D card
(pages 110–111)
*and* hanging felt stars
(pages 46–49)

(cut out centre)

**pompom disc**
(pages 10–11)
cut two in cardboard

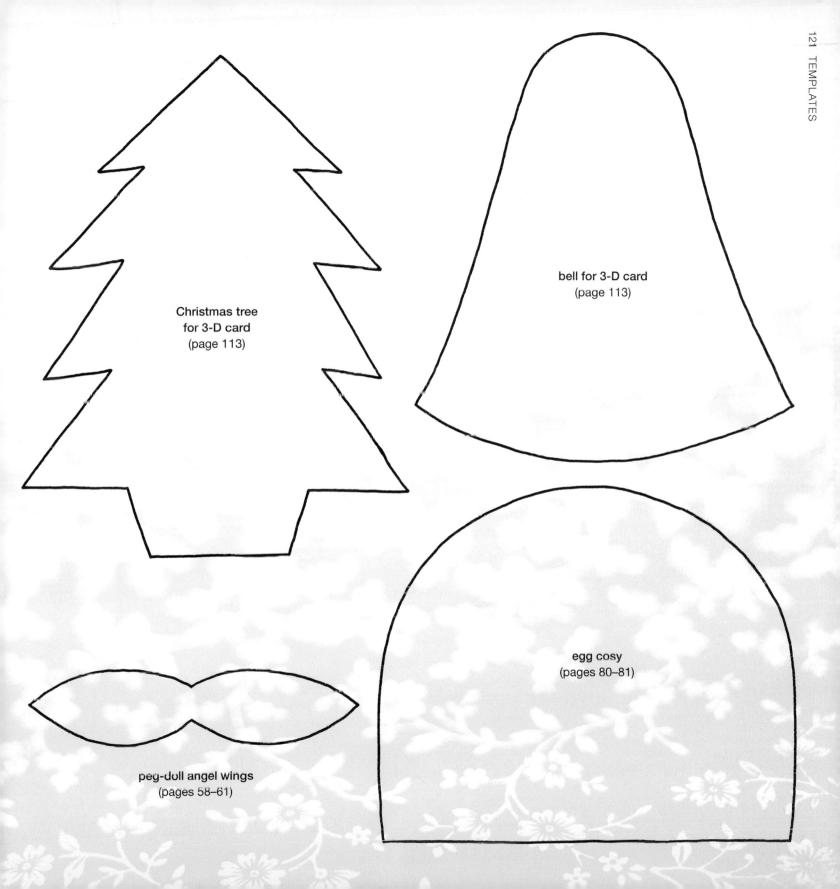

Christmas tree
for 3-D card
(page 113)

bell for 3-D card
(page 113)

egg cosy
(pages 80–81)

peg-doll angel wings
(pages 58–61)

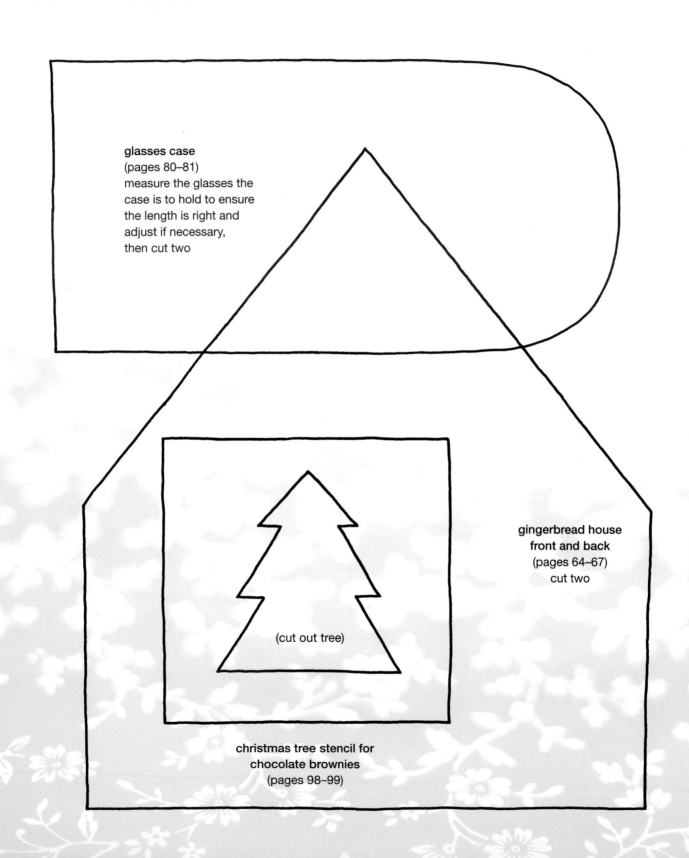

**glasses case**
(pages 80–81)
measure the glasses the
case is to hold to ensure
the length is right and
adjust if necessary,
then cut two

**gingerbread house
front and back**
(pages 64–67)
cut two

(cut out tree)

**christmas tree stencil for
chocolate brownies**
(pages 98–99)

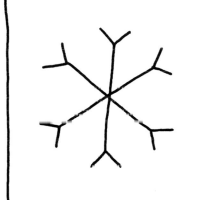

snowflake motif for
tealight holder
(pages 62–63)

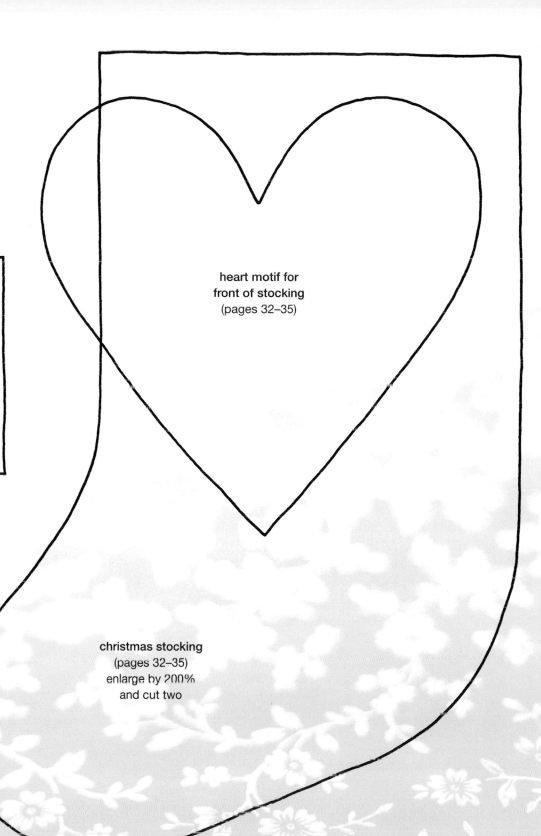

heart motif for
front of stocking
(pages 32–35)

christmas stocking
(pages 32–35)
enlarge by 200%
and cut two

# sources

### CALICO CRAFTS
www.calicocrafts.co.uk
*Online crafts specialist
with large stock of crafting
materials. Also vintage-style
labels that are ideal for
découpage projects.*

### CREATIONS ART AND
### CRAFTS MATERIALS
01326 555777
www.ecreations.co.uk
*Online craft store with large
stock of air-drying modelling
clay in a wide variety of
colours, Christmas-themed
rubber stamps and stencils,
paints, glue and more.*

### EARLY LEARNING
### CENTRE
Call 0870 535 2352 or visit
www.elc.co.uk for details
of your nearest store.
*Their large craft section*

*includes funky-coloured
paints, different-sized
paintbrushes, felt-tip pens,
scissors, glitter pens, glue,
pompoms, coloured feathers
and simple stencils – great
for younger children who
enjoy art and craft.*

### CREATIVE BEADCRAFT
1 Marshall Street
London W1F 9BA
020 7734 1982
www.creativebeadcraft.co.uk
*Huge selection of beads
including wood, glass,
rocaille, pearl and crystal
designs, as well as feathers,
sequins and tiny glass beads
in numerous colours.*

### THE ENGLISH STAMP
### COMPANY
www.englishstamp.com
*Traditional wooden stamps,
including a good selection
of Christmassy stamps in
simple Shaker-style designs
and various sizes. Also ink
pads in a large range of
colours, including metallics
and inks that can be
stamped on glass.*

### GREAT LITTLE
### TRADING CO.
Call 0870 850 6000 or visit
www.gltc.co.uk for a
catalogue.

*A wide selection of ready-
mixed paint, art folders and
fun craft kits for kids.*

### HOBBYCRAFT
0800 027 2387
Visit www.hobbycraft.co.uk
for details of your nearest
store.
*Nationwide chain of craft
superstores, carrying
everything that the young
crafter needs: ribbons,
pompoms, air-drying clay,
googly eyes, Fimo modelling
clay, blank cards and
envelopes, Christmas stamps
and ink stamp pads, sequins,
buttons and beads, plus
much more.*

### HOMECRAFTS DIRECT
0116 269 7733
www.homecrafts.co.uk
*Log on here to order hard-to-
find items such as tinsel pipe*

*cleaners, plain wooden
frames and cracker snaps,
as well as all the necessary
craft staples, including crêpe
paper, plain and coloured
doilies, glue sticks, glue
guns, fabric paints, air-drying
clay, Fimo modelling clay,
ready-to-decorate face
masks and instant papier-
mâché mix.*

### IKEA
Visit www.ikea.com for a
catalogue or details of your
nearest store.
*Good selection of wooden
boxes and files and plain
picture frames in unfinished
wood that are ready for
painting and decorating. Also
seasonal selections of fun
decorations, wrapping paper
and cards.*

### JANE ASHER PARTY
### CAKES AND SUGARCRAFT
24 Cale Street
London SW3 3QU
020 7584 6177
www.jane-asher.co.uk
*Excellent selection of novelty-
shaped cookie cutters (some
with festive motifs) in both
metal and plastic, plus cake
decorations, cake frills, a
variety of pretty paper doilies
and coloured cake cases in
many different sizes.*

## JOHN LEWIS

Visit www.johnlewis.com for details of your nearest store. *John Lewis haberdashery departments offer embroidery threads and cottons in many colours, as well as other craft essentials including felt, pipe cleaners, craft fabrics, a variety of ribbons, ricrac braid, beaded trims, buttons and sequins. Also kids' crafting kits such as Hama beads.*

## LETTERBOX

Visit www.letterbox.co.uk to order a catalogue. *Creative and educational toys including art and craft kits that make ideal Christmas gifts for keen little crafters, including a peg-doll and a beading kit as well as starter sewing kits.*

## LITTLE CRAFTYBUGS

www.littlecraftybugs.co.uk *Online supplier of a huge range of craft supplies and kids for keen junior crafters, including a special selection that's devoted entirely to Christmas crafting.*

## MACCULLOCH & WALLIS

25–26 Dering Street
London W1 1AT
020 7629 0311
www.macculloch-wallis.co.uk
*Vast selection of fabrics, including boiled wool, wool and felt, as well as lace, ribbons and ricrac and other braids sold by the metre. They also stock cute novelty buttons, zips, appliqué motifs and sewing cottons.*

## PAPERCHASE

213 Tottenham Court Road
London W1T 7PS
020 7467 6200
Visit www.paperchase.co.uk for details of your nearest store.
*Large selection of hand-made papers, crêpe and tissue paper and metallic card, fabric-covered books and photograph albums. Also 3-D paint, glitter glue pens, and blank cards and envelopes in many colours and sizes.*

## REDICUT ONLINE

www.readicut.co.uk
*Large selection of specialist paper-crafting equipment, including papers, punches, stamps, inks, stamping pads, stencils, découpage papers, cutters, ribbons and other embellishments.*

## SELWYN-SMITH STUDIOS

148 High Street
Teddington
Middlesex TW11 8HZ
020 8973 0771
*Paper, pens, pencils, brushes and paint dishes.*

## THE STENCIL LIBRARY

Stocksfield Hall
Northumberland
NE43 7TN
01661 844 844
www.stencil-library.com
*Decorative stencils, from simple festive shapes to more complicated designs, plus stencil paints, sponges and brushes. Their paints can be used on walls, furniture and fabrics.*

## VV ROULEAUX

102 Marylebone Lane
London W1U 2QD
020 7224 5179
Visit www.vvrouleaux.com for details of their other stores.
*A vast selection of ribbons*

*from taffeta and velvet to embroidered cotton, plus pompoms, feathered trims, pretty braids and silk flowers.*

## THE WIMBLEDON SEWING & CRAFT SUPERSTORE

296–312 Balham High Road
London SW17 7AA
020 8767 0036
www.craftysewer.com
*Everything from beads and sequins to blank metallic card, felt, pompoms, wool, buttons and pipe cleaners.*

## WOOLWORTHS

www.woolworths.co.uk
*Now an online supplier of kids' craft materials. Their large selection includes paper, paints, felt tips, 3-D paint pens, glitter glue and assorted collage materials, as well as crafting essentials such as cutting boards, scissors and rulers.*

# picture credits

ALL PHOTOGRAPHY BY POLLY WREFORD

Pages 2–3 air-drying clay, glitter and ribbon from Hobbycraft, paintbrushes from The Wimbledon Sewing & Craft Superstore; pages 4–5 wool fabric, gingham, thread and mother-of-pearl button from The Wimbledon Sewing & Craft Superstore; pages 6–7 air-drying clay, paint, spotted felt and sequins all from Hobbycraft, wooden frame from IKEA, paper doilies and blank greetings cards from Lakeland Ltd, ricrac trim from John Lewis; pages 8–9 silver card, wool, pipe cleaners and glitter all from The Wimbledon Sewing & Craft Superstore; mistletoe lights from a selection by Lakeland Ltd; pages 10–11 wool, gingham ribbon and 3-D fabric pen from The Wimbledon Sewing & Craft Superstore, white twigs from Lalage Barran Flowers; pages 12–13 wool, felt, pipe cleaners and 3-D fabric pens all from The Wimbledon Sewing & Craft Superstore, gingham ribbon from VV Rouleaux; pages 14–15 cinnamon sticks from Sainsbury's, gingham ribbon from VV Rouleaux, artificial Christmas tree from Bloom, bells from The Wimbledon Sewing & Craft Superstore; pages 16–17 white paper from Paperchase, bedlinen from a selection at Cath Kidston; pages 18–19 oranges from Sainsbury's, gingham ribbon from VV Rouleaux, fresh Christmas tree from Lalage Barran Flowers; pages 20–21 artificial mini tree from a selection at Selfridges, candy canes from Lidl, gingham ribbons from VV Rouleaux, terracotta pot from Homebase, silver paint, sparkly pompoms and silver ribbon all from The Wimbledon Sewing & Craft Superstore; pages 22–23 as above; pages 24–25 metallic wrapping paper from Paperchase, pink and silver sequinned braid from The Wimbledon Sewing & Craft Superstore; pages 26–27 Fimo modelling clay and decorative gold dust from The Wimbledon Sewing & Craft Superstore; pages 28–29 as above; pages 30–31 glycerine from Sainsburys, distilled water available from chemists or hardware stores, Christmas figures, silver paint, brushes and glitter all from The Wimbledon Sewing & Craft Superstore; pages 32–33 cream wool fabric, gingham, button and embroidery wool all from The Wimbledon Sewing & Craft Superstore, red spotted felt from Hobbycraft; pages 34–35 as above; pages 36–37 silver card, wool for pompom, glue, metallic pipe cleaners and glitter all from The Wimbledon Sewing & Craft Superstore, artificial tree from Bloom; pages 38–39 as above; pages 40–41 metallic wrapping paper from Paperchase; pages 42–43 air-drying clay from Hobbycraft, cookie cutters from Jane Asher Party Cakes, glue, ribbon and ribbons all from The Wimbledon Sewing & Craft Superstore, artificial tree from Bloom; pages 44–45 air-drying clay from Hobbycraft, paint and sequins and sheer ribbon all from The Wimbledon Sewing & Craft Superstore, wrapping paper from Paperchase, coloured string from a selection at IKEA; pages 46–47 felt and ricrac braid from The Wimbledon Sewing & Craft Superstore, mother-of-pearl buttons from John Lewis; pages 48–49 as above; pages 50–51 rocaille glass beads, wire and silver ribbon all from The Wimbledon Sewing & Craft Superstore, silver wrapping paper from John Lewis; pages 52–53 silver and gold paint, glitter, bells and ribbon all from The Wimbledon Sewing & Craft Superstore; pages 54–55 wrapping paper from John Lewis; sequins and ribbons from The Wimbledon Sewing & Craft superstore; pages 56–57 as above; pages 58–59 paper doilies from Lakeland Ltd, silver card and metallic pipe cleaners from The Wimbledon Sewing & Craft Superstore, wooden pegs from Hobbycraft; page 60–61 as above; pages 62–63 glass votives from IKEA; 3-D fabric pens from The Wimbledon Sewing & Craft Superstore, coloured tealights from Homebase; pages 64–65 tubes of icing and ingredients from Sainsbury's, candy canes from Lidl; pages 66–67 as above; pages 68–69 florist's wire hoop and twigs from Lalage Barran, silver and gold paint and ribbons all from The Wimbledon Sewing & Craft Superstore; pages 70–71 craft papers from The Wimbledon Sewing & Craft Superstore; pages 72–73 ribbons and tissue paper from Hobbycraft; pages 74–75 as above; page 76–77 cellophane and air-drying clay from Hobbycraft, ribbon from VV Rouleaux, wrapping paper from a selection at IKEA; pages 78–79 terracotta pots from Homebase, silver paint and sheer ribbon from The Wimbledon Sewing & Craft Superstore, pillar candles from Colony; pages 80–81 spotted felt from Hobbycraft; felt ricrac trim from a selection at IKEA, embroidery cotton from The Wimbledon Sewing & Craft Superstore; pages 82–83 ready-rolled icing and cupcake cases from Jane Asher Party Cakes, tissue paper from Hobbycraft; pages 84–85 spotted felt from Hobbycraft; plain felt and embroidery cotton from The Wimbledon Sewing & Craft Superstore; mother-of-pearl star-shaped buttons and egg cups from John Lewis; pages 86–87 red ribbon from The Wimbledon Sewing & Craft Superstore, cloves available from supermarkets and food stores; pages 88–89 ingredients available from supermarkets and food stores, tissue paper from Hobbycraft, decorations from a selection at Paperchase; pages 90–91 wool fabric and wool thread from The Wimbledon Sewing & Craft Superstore, silver ricrac from Paperchase, silver/white felt from Hobbycraft; pages 92–93 green wool fabric from The Wimbledon Sewing & Craft Superstore, silver ricrac from Paperchase, silver/white felt from Hobbycraft; pages 94–95 terracotta pot from a selection at Homebase, red felt decoration from a selection at Paperchase, red ricrac braid and silver paint from The Wimbledon Sewing & Craft Superstore, bulbs from Lalage Barran; pages 96–97 ingredients available from supermarkets and food stores; pages 98–99 patterned découpage papers and paint from The Wimbledon Sewing & Craft Superstore, tissue paper from Hobbycraft, tin from Sainsbury's; pages 100–101 blank cards from Lakeland Ltd and Paperchase; patterned wrapping paper from Paperchase, felt from Hobbycraft; pages 102–103 cookie cutters from Jane Asher Party Cakes, sheer ribbons from Hobbycraft; pages 104–105 blank cards and bag from a selection at Paperchase, silver paint and glitter from The Wimbledon Sewing & Craft Superstore; pages 106–107 red card from Hobbycraft, stamp from The English Stamp Company; pages 108–109 blank cards from Hobbycraft, gingham wallpaper from Designers Guild; pages 110–111 blank cards and pink/silver wrapping paper from Paperchase, metallic gold and silver papers, ribbons and sequins all from The Wimbledon Sewing & Craft Superstore; pages 112–113 blank cards from Paperchase, red spotted felt from Hobbycraft; pages 114–115 blank cards from Hobbycraft, felt and glitter from The Wimbledon Sewing & Craft Superstore; pages 116–117 wrapping paper from IKEA; stencil and red gingham ribbon from The Wimbledon Sewing & Craft Superstore.

# index

3-D Christmas cards 110–11

**A**

angels
    angel tree topper 36–9
    peg-doll angel 58–61

**B**

bags
    book bag 92–3
    stamped gift bag 106
    stencilled gift bag 118–19
beaded decorations 50–51
bells
    blue 113
    festive 52–3
biscuits, cinnamon 72–5
blue bells 113
book bag 92–3
bulbs, planted 96–7
button photo frame 86–7

**C**

candle centrepiece 78–9
candy canes 20, 21, 119
cards
    3-D Christmas 110–11
    blue bells 113
    Christmas trees 116–17
    felt motif 114–15
    glitter stars 117
    glittery trees 113
    gold and silver hearts 112
    holly 107
chocolate brownies 98–9
Christmas cards, 3-D 110–11
Christmas crackers 54–7
Christmas stocking 30–35
cinnamon
    biscuits 72–5
    sticks 14–15
clay decorations 42–5

coconut ice 90–91
crackers, Christmas 54–7
cushion 94–5

**D E**

découpaged tin 100–101
egg cosy, felt 84–5

**F**

Father Christmas
    peg doll 59
    tree decoration 13
    tree topper 39
felt egg cosy 84–5
felt motif cards 114–15
festive bells 52–3

**G H**

gift tags
    stamped 108–9
    star 45
gingerbread house 64–7
glasses case 80–81
glitter stars 117
glittery trees 113
gold and silver hearts 112
hanging felt stars 46–9
holly cards 107

**L M**

lanterns, paper 24–5
mini tree 20–23

**N O**

nativity scene 26–9
orange pomanders 88–9
orange tree decorations
    18–19

**P**

paper lanterns 24–5
paper snowflakes 16–17
paperchains 40–41
peg dolls
    Father Christmas 59
    peg-doll angel 58–61

peppermint creams 82–3
photo frame, button 86–7
planted bulbs 96–7
pomanders 88–9
pompom tree decorations
    10–13
    angel tree topper 36–9
    Father Christmas 13
    making pompoms 10
    miniature 20, 21, 22
    robin 13
    snowmen 12
pot pourri 76–7
potato print wrapping paper
    104–5

**R S**

robin tree decoration 13
Rudolf the reindeer tree
    topper 39
scented gifts
    lavender-scented felt
        shapes 48
    tealight holders 62–3
snow globes 30–31
snowflakes, paper 16–17
snowmen
    peppermint creams 82–3
    tree decoration 12
sources 124–5
stamped gift bag 106
stamped gift tags 108–9
stars
    3-D Christmas cards
        110–11
    glitter 117
    hanging felt 46–9
    star gift tag 45
stencilled gift bag 118–19

**T**

tealight holders 62–3
templates 120–23
    bell for 3-D card 121
    Christmas stocking 123
    Christmas tree for 3-D

card 121
Christmas tree stencil for
    chocolate brownies
    122
egg cosy 121
gingerbread house 122
glasses case 122
heart for 3-D card 120
heart motif for front of
    stocking 123
peg-doll angel wings 121
pompom disc 120
small heart for centre of
    3-D card 120
snowflake motif for
    tealight holder 123
star for 3-D card and
    hanging felt stars 120
tin, découpaged 100–101
tree decorations
    beaded 50–51
    Father Christmas 13
    making pompoms 10
    miniature pompoms 20,
        21, 22
    orange 18–19
    robin 13
    snowmen 12
tree toppers
    angel 36–9
    Father Christmas 39
    gingham ribbon 22
    Rudolf the reindeer 39
trees
    Christmas 116–17
    glittery 113
    mini tree 20–23
twiggy wreath 68–9

**W**

wrapping paper, potato print
    104–5
wreath, twiggy 68–9

# acknowledgments

Thank you to Polly Wreford for her beautiful photography and attention to detail in the wonderful pictures she shot for the book. Thanks to Toni Kay and Annabel Morgan for their help during all stages of the book – its design, layout and words. Thank you to all the fantastic children who modelled for us – for their patience during photography, and their enthusiasm for the projects they worked on. Thanks to my daughters – to Jessica for designing and making the nativity scene, and to Anna for helping to make some of the nativity scene animals. Thanks are also due to Hobbycraft, for supplying their wonderful ribbons, card and felt, and to The English Stamp Company for supplying the wooden stamps. Finally a big thank you to my husband Michael, for his unfailing support and encouragement.

Ryland Peters & Small would like to thank all the children who modelled for this book, including Aimee, Alessandra, Alissia, Amelia, Anna, Archie, Ayesha, Cameron, Chantal, Donnell-Andre, Hannah, Hassia, Honor, Jack, Jago, Jessica, Kai, Saskia, Tom, Tommy and William.